A SPIRIT DAUGHTER
WORKBOOK

---

written by
Jill Wintersteen

FOR THE FULL MOON &
PENUMBRAL LUNAR ECLIPSE
Friday, January 10th
11:21AM PST

WHY THE LUNAR ECLIPSE

At the start of a new decade, we are greeted by a Lunar Eclipse in Cancer, opening a doorway for release and the realization of our true potential. This Lunar Eclipse is a follow up to the Solar Eclipse on the New Moon in Capricorn. Both Eclipses work together to help us bridge the visions created on the New Moon and the actual manifestation of our dreams. Full Moons help us breakdown barriers that prevent us from attracting the energies needed to embody our intentions. They often bring up a perceived crisis, where our emotions intensify until we feel an energetic shift leading us towards a new path and new way of being. A Lunar Eclipse amplifies these already existing Full Moon vibrations and provides an even greater opportunity for release and transformation.

On a Full Moon, the Sun and Moon stand in full opposition of one another. Additionally, they each sit in opposing zodiac constellations, activating that sign's energy and illuminating it in our lives. This Lunar Eclipse, the qualities governed by Capricorn and Cancer are felt more deeply in our energetic and emotional body. They become more accessible to us and highlighted in our consciousness. We can more easily feel and work with them to create breakthroughs in our lives.

We also have the influence of the Lunar Nodes adding to the existing power of this Full Moon. The Sun and Moon's proximity to Lunar Nodes is what causes an Eclipse. Lunar Eclipses occur on a Full Moon when the Sun is near one Lunar Node and the Moon near another. The North and South Lunar Node exist at the point where the Sun's path crosses the Moon's orbit in our sky. Their crossing creates an energetic vortex just as powerful as any cosmic body, even though they are not physical in nature. Lunar Nodes have just as much impact on our frequency as physical cosmic bodies, displaying the magic of the universe.

Lunar Nodes, like the planets, also fall against astrological constellations, taking on their energy. They shift zodiac signs every eighteen months, changing the placements of our Eclipses. Currently, the North Node is in Cancer, and the South Node is in Capricorn. The North Node's energy is where society is heading. It brings us the lessons we are ready to master as a collective. It also shows us a potential path forward for humanity if we choose to walk that path together. The North Node in Cancer asks us to spend more time nourishing our soul and restoring our energy. It emphasizes the importance of aligning with our intuition and taking a softer approach to decision making. Cancer is the great mother of the zodiac, and with the North Node here, we are brought situations that guide us to be more compassionate with ourselves and others.

The South Node's energy is what we are leaving behind as a society, especially the lower vibrations of the sign. It is what we have already mastered as a collective and what we are shifting away from in the coming years. The South Node in Capricorn asks us to put down our workaholic ways and spend more time enjoying life. This placement emphasizes the importance of feeling good while feeling productive and urges us to give up the notion that we must struggle to be successful. It also asks us to step away from overly logical solutions which feel misaligned with our heart.

With the North Node in Cancer and the South Node in Capricorn, we are asked to create a greater balance in our life between our intuitive and our logical side. It asks us to redefine our life to include more restoration, more joy, and more healing. The Lunar Eclipse helps us embrace these energies on a collective level, helping each of us transition from one state of being to another. When we all align with the energy of the cosmos, we can create powerful shifts throughout all of society. We unify and encourage changes in old paradigms as we all take on a new perspective. As you work with these energies, look outside yourself and offer help to others in understanding the cosmic vibrations affecting all of us. Connect the dots from you to another and see yourself reflected in everyone you meet. Know that we are all making this shift as a collective and encourage the energies emerging to manifest throughout your life.

CANCER LUNAR ECLIPSE

When the Lunar Eclipse meets Cancer, magic is in the air. Ruled by the Moon and the element of water, Cancer amplifies the already feminine and nurturing powers of the Moon. Their meeting sets the stage for great healing and opens the doorway for our most intuitive self to shine through. This may be the most emotionally intense Full Moon all year, as Cancer asks us to hold space for our deepest feelings. She encourages emotions to rise to the surface of our consciousness, where we can release, shift, and transform them into places of power.

The energy of Cancer is fluid and capable of significant change. She softens the structure brought to us in Capricorn Season and asks where we can create space for healing. This time of year brings about long to-do lists and a series of goals to meet. Cancer encourages us to step away from our expectations to feel. She has no use for time or neatly organized calendar blocks as her work has no timeline. She asks us to be completely present with ourselves and allow energies to unfold rather than forcing them. She reminds us to cultivate patience and not to rush our healing but rather to understand that our emotions are a process which requires nurturing, not direction.

Throughout this Lunar Eclipse, give yourself space to feel. Let down any walls you've built around your most tender areas and be vulnerable to your emotions. Raw emotions are not always easy to digest, but this Moon is the time to give them the nourishment of an open heart. You do not need to force emotions to come out. If you do notice feelings wanting to surface, give them your full attention. We often suppress our emotions, or distract ourselves from them in some manner. Recognize the ways you might prevent your emotions from fully emerging, and instead soften your approach. Quietly listen to your feelings without judgment, and let them show you the way to healing. Speak directly to your emotions, first acknowledging them and letting them know they are heard. Then thank them for showing up and allowing you to shift them.

As you sit with some of your deepest feelings, know they are temporary. They will pass, even if they feel permanent in the moment. As you bring awareness to them, they will naturally release and you will feel energetically lighter. They will also open the doorway to your intuition. If we suppress our feelings, we become unable to access our intuition. We then get lost in a sea of logic and practicalities, forgetting the answers we seek lie just beneath the emotions we are trying to avoid. Our intuition is the prize for the uncomfortableness of feeling at our deepest level. Once we learn to be patient with our emotions and give them unrestricted space, we can feel our way through life lead by our highest intuitive guidance.

Our intuition then directs our healing, showing us paths we wouldn't find with logic alone. It can also help us understand where to focus our energy. The Capricorn New Moon asked us to identify what was really worth our energy. This Lunar Eclipse is the second part of that question, asking us what depletes our energy, and how can we restore it? Often, unresolved emotions deplete and distract us form our true focus. They undermine our greatest efforts to change or to create our best life. These emotions may be conscious or subconscious, but their effect is the same: they keep us stuck in a perpetual loop of creating intentions but not being able to manifest them into reality. If you feel blocked, no matter how many intentions you set, try asking your intuition where healing is needed. Hold space for the emotions that need attention knowing that when you do, they pass, and your path forward becomes clear.

As you work with the energy of this Lunar Eclipse, ask yourself how you can truly nurture yourself. What restores your energy, and what depletes it? Release anything you no longer want. Know, though, that to truly let go of an energy, you need to understand it. Also bring new understanding to your joy, love, and other positive emotions. You always have the power to choose what you want to feel in any moment. This choice becomes more clear when you understand all of your emotions. As you sit with your emotions this Lunar Eclipse, feel your intuition surface. Allow it to lead and soften you as you take a break from the energy of Capricorn and dive deeply into the flow of your energy.

CANCER MOON X CAPRICORN SUN

Cancer governs the fourth house of the zodiac, this is the house of the home. It represents our physical home but also our energetic, emotional home. The fourth house is the lowest point on the zodiac wheel and represents our most subjective, internalized energies. It is here we bury our deepest fears, our greatest desires, and every subconscious energy which alters our perceptions and perspectives. The fourth house, and the energy of Cancer, helps us define our home frequency. This vibration determines what we attract, what we manifest, and what we emit out into the world. It is also the place we return to when we are thrown from our center, as it represents our deepest roots and the pieces of our soul that need nourishment and compassion in our darkest hours.

Capricorn, in opposition, is home to the tenth house of the zodiac, known as the house of career. It represents our interactions with the world and our reputation, or what we are known for in this life. The tenth house sits at the very top of the zodiac wheel and represents our most objective world. This house, and the energy of Capricorn, helps us merge the person we are at our roots with the person we show to the rest of the world. Capricorn, like Cancer, helps us return to our core. We can always align with Capricorn to return home and ensure that the frequency we are emitting outward is truly reflection our soul.

Opposing signs are always similar in nature, but their execution of the energy is different. On this Lunar Eclipse, we have the opportunity to work with both of these energies, to shed their lower vibrations, and to integrate their higher frequencies into our energetic body. In addition, these astrological energies are enhanced by the Lunar Eclipse. We have a greater opportunity this day to detach from energies, not serving us and embrace vibrations that align with our best self. Both Cancer and Capricorn are concerned with our responsibilities. Where Cancer is focused on our responsibility to ourselves, Capricorn is focused on our responsibilities to other people and society in general. Cancer asks us always to remember that our energy is precious and needs tending, time to restore, and space to heal. Our greatest responsibility in this lifetime is to ensure we are taken care of, and our soul is fulfilled. We also have an obligation to our intuition, which includes taking time to hear it and taking chances to follow it, for it is our ultimate guiding light.

CANCER MOON X CAPRICORN SUN

Capricorn asks us to focus on how we are influencing the energy around us through our focus and life's work. Capricorn reminds us that we have a responsibility in this life to understand ourselves so we can share our greatest gifts with others. This sharing is often done through our career or life's work. When we fully embody the highest vibrations of Capricorn, we align our work with our core frequency and find pure joy. We emit this joy everywhere we go and influence those around us through our energy. We encourage others to align with their soul, and we help change the world together through our collective responsibility to honor our core values.

To fully align with the higher vibrations of Cancer and Capricorn, we must release their lower vibrations. These are the extreme, or shadow, sides of the sign. They show us the places where we need compassion and attention to shift our energy.

The low side of Cancer can cause us to become emotionally dependent on others. When we align with this side of Cancer, we need other people to help us contain our emotions, forgetting that it is our responsibility to take care of them, not others. This low vibration may show up as oversharing our feelings when it is inappropriate or to an unsupportive audience. It can also manifest as a lack of compassion for ourselves as we expect others to tend to our feelings, but forget to acknowledge them ourselves. The low side of Cancer can swing to the opposite extreme as well. When we align with this side, we numb our emotions and suppress them. We find whatever means necessary to avoid feeling them. We forget our responsibility to nurture feelings and hold space for them. Both sides of Cancer's low vibrations cause us to disconnect from our intuition and step away from ourselves- our home.

The low vibrations of Capricorn show up as judgment of ourselves and judgment of others. The two go hand in hand, as our judgment of the people around us, is merely a reflection of our own self-judgment. There are a myriad of reasons why we may judge ourselves. On this Lunar Eclipse, look at the ways you may lack compassion for yourself and judge your thoughts, behaviors, and even feelings. Often judgment comes from a sense of misalignment with our core values. When we feel out of integrity or unhappy with the way we are showing up in the world, we end up feeling insecure. Insecurity leads to judgment of others, as we try to find ways to make ourselves feel better. Instead of judging others, or yourself, consider developing ways to make yourself feel more secure. Start by aligning your life with what resonates with you on a soul level. Take the time to understand yourself this Lunar Eclipse, along with your emotions, so that you can create a life that embodies your true essence. When we align our life with our soul, we naturally feel more secure and instantly move away from the lower vibration of judgment.

As you work with the energies of this Lunar Eclipse, remain focused on holding space to develop a deeper understanding of your energy. This space involves nurturing your emotions, developing your intuition, and releasing judgment of yourself and others. Have compassion for yourself as you learn to restore your energy before directing it. When we combine the higher vibrations of Cancer and Capricorn, we create a balanced life, where we allow ourselves to feel every emotion, including joy, while following our intuition. We lead ourselves from our heart into making choices aligned with our soul, which become our life's work. We uphold the responsibility to ourselves and others with grace and ease as we share our gifts freely with the world.

CANCER ASPECTS

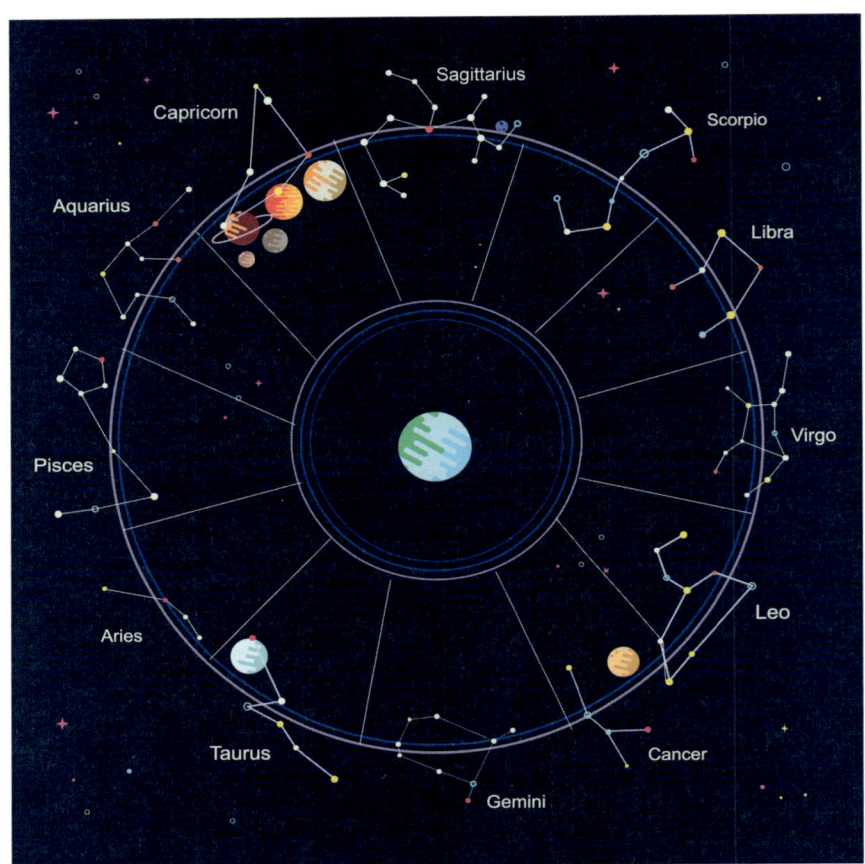

Aspects are additional energetic influences from other cosmic bodies on the Full Moon. The main aspect of any Full Moon is the opposition of the Sun and the Moon. Oppositions allow us to fully view both energies involved. They often bring subconscious patterns and emotions to the surface, creating a perceived crisis that leads to an energetic breakthrough. We have quite a few more planets and their energies involved on this Eclipse, including more oppositions. This Eclipse proves to be full of opportunity for shifts in consciousness if we allow the energies to be felt, seen, and transformed into something else. This shift requires our awareness, our willingness to go through the process of exploring ourselves, and the desire to detach from what holds us back from our healing.

Joining the Sun and the South Lunar Node in Capricorn are Mercury, Saturn, Pluto, and Jupiter. Mercury, Saturn, and Pluto are all conjunct, or next to, the Sun, which means they also directly oppose the Moon. Jupiter is conjunct the South Node and directly opposes the North Node in Cancer.

CANCER ASPECTS

Mercury is the planet of communication, it rules how we exchange energy with ourselves and others. Mercury's involvement on this Eclipse challenges our internal dialogue. It's a time to look at your inner verbiage and ask yourself if it matches up with your true feelings. Also, ask if it supports and nourishes you, facilitating healing, or does it deplete or undermine your intentions. The way we speak to ourselves is important in creating energetic shifts. Some of this speech may be conscious, while some may be subconscious. Spend some time listening to yourself and notice the way you speak to yourself. Is it energizing or depleting? Is it supportive or counterproductive? Furthermore, is it nurturing and compassionate?

Saturn is the planet of responsibility. It is the ruler of Capricorn and inspires us to make commitments with the understanding of long term consequences. Its a rather serious energy, which can be internalized as pressure. If worries around your commitments or responsibilities arise this Eclipse, know it is Saturn bringing your awareness to them. While evaluating these things is always a good exercise, try not to force any answers. Also, try not to succumb to the pressure of time. Know that everything unfolds at the right moment when it's meant to be. Continue to nurture what you love by making commitments aligned with your intuition. Hear your soul speak this Eclipse and know that your only responsibility is to follow it. Release all of your "what ifs" and trust the timing of your life.

Pluto is the planet of rebirth and transformation. Pluto's energy reveals buried emotions and energies so they can be transmuted into power. Pluto helps us understand the ongoing cycles of our energy over many lifetimes and reminds us that we are far more powerful than we could ever imagine. Feel the influence of this vibration challenging you to hold space for your pain so it can no longer contain you. Pluto's energy has the ability to destroy old versions, one's which block our growth and evolution. On this Eclipse, surrender your attachments to the person who you once were and embrace the new one. Feel into your new truth rising above the ashes of the emotions revealed and transformed this Eclipse.

Jupiter joins Mercury, Saturn, and Pluto in Capricorn. Jupiter brings the energy of expansion to this Eclipse. It encourages us to widen our view to include a different perspective of old energies. How can you see the same emotion differently? How can you interpret its meaning differently? Jupiter's placement next to the South Node inspires us to take a leap of faith and follow our intuition over our logic. It's encouraging us to expand past our old ways of doing things and embrace a new future defined by an integration between what brings us joy and what brings us success.

The other significant influence today is Uranus stationing direct in Taurus, ushering in a period when all planets are moving forward. When all planets are moving direct, it brings us motivation and eagerness to get things started. It's a wonderful time to begin new projects or pick up ones that have been forgotten. It may also feel like the world is moving quickly around you, and it's challenging to keep up. Find some time to ground your energy today and become clear on which direction you want to pursue. As you unblock yourself through emotional work, get ready for the energy to flow, and flow quickly. Now is the time to expect changes to occur overnight and see measurable shifts in your energy and the energy you're attracting. We will continue this forward motion until Mercury Retrograde on February 17th. Until then, enjoy the free-flowing current ready to pick you up and take you as far as your dreams allow.

NODESCOPES

On the Lunar Eclipse, we have an opportunity to work with our personal Lunar Nodes in addition to the collective Lunar Nodes. We each have a North and South Node position in our natal chart. This is the place where the Nodes were located when you were born. The South Node represents energies you have already mastered in a previous life. They feel comfortable to you and can become limiting comfort zones if you aren't aware of any attachments to them. The North Node represents lessons you are here to learn in this lifetime. They are energies which, at first, feel foreign to you and even difficult to understand. They may challenge you on several levels, and you may initially resist allowing them into your life. It's important to be open to the lessons of your North Node. This is the place where you can evolve, grow and see your potential.

On the Eclipse, we have an opportunity to release the lower vibrations of our South Node and step away from any comfort zones it may be forming in our lives. We also have the opportunity to embrace and understand our North Node as we integrate its energies on a deeper level. Below are suggestions on where to focus the energy of this Lunar Eclipse based on your personal Lunar Nodes. You can look up your Nodes at astro-charts.com. Your South Node is always directly opposite your North Node.

Aries North Node | Libra South Node:
Your journey this lifetime is to embrace your own path, independent of others. With Libra in your South Node, it is natural for you to seek out partnerships. They feel comfortable to you, and while having relationships is important, your focus this Lunar Eclipse is on yourself. Nurture your feelings around partnerships and release any notions that you need others to feel complete. Embrace your personal journey and know that some parts you may need to walk alone.

Taurus North Node | Scorpio South Node:
Your journey this lifetime is to tend to your roots and grow. With your South Node in Scorpio, destruction is your comfort zone. You feel most at home when in a state of transformation, and may become addicted to the struggle of change. While working on yourself is good, too much can lead to feeling ungrounded as you continually transform to the next version, never enjoying your current state. On the Eclipse, feel the perfection of where you are right now. Nurture the person who you are today and give them space to bloom.

Gemini North Node | Sagittarius South Node:
Your journey this lifetime is to work with the details of life. With your South Node in Sagittarius, you take comfort in the bigger picture, always viewing the world through a wide-angle lens. You love to travel, yearning for the freedom of the open road. Your work, though, is to stay long enough in one place to gather as much information as possible. On this Eclipse, lay down some roots and spend time asking yourself the harder questions. Stay long enough for the answers and then connect the dots between the details of your deepest emotions.

Cancer North Node | Capricorn South Node
You are astrologically aligned with this Eclipse and may feel it on a deeper level than most. Your journey this lifetime is to feel. With your South Node in Capricorn, your comfort zone may be work or your career. You may even find yourself forgoing some of life's sweetest moments for a chance of success and recognition. Your challenge this lifetime is to heal. Capricorn in the South Node represents hardships in a previous life. On this Eclipse, shift your focus to feeling good and finding ways to clear the past from your frequency. You no longer need to struggle, choose joy instead.

Leo North Node | Aquarius South Node
Your journey this lifetime is to speak from the heart. With your South Node in Aquarius, you rely heavily on your intellect, especially when speaking to the collective. Your comfort zones lie within pushing boundaries, and you are always looking for a new solution to an old problem. This Eclipse challenge yourself to feel your heart speak. Learn how to express it, first to yourself, then to others. Realize that when you move from a place of compassion and vulnerability, you lead others through your example. This action will make the change you desire to see in the world.

NODESCOPES

Virgo North Node | Pisces North Node

Your journey this lifetime is to heal, then to be of service to others in their healing. With your South Node in Pisces, you hold a vast array of universal knowledge. You could spend a lifetime unraveling the mysteries of human consciousness. You find comfort in your daydreams and tend to escape to alternate realities when available. Challenge yourself this Eclipse to stay present with your emotions. As you spend time with them, find ways to organize your knowledge so others may understand it. You hold great power once you learn how to share your energy with the world.

Libra North Node | Aries South Node

Your journey this lifetime is to understand, and embrace, partnerships. With your South Node in Aries, your natural tendency is to walk your path alone. You find comfort in putting yourself first and can find it challenging to be in relationships. You may resist them, until you are ready to step into an unknown part of yourself and learn to experience life with others. On this Eclipse, feel your emotions around partnerships. Be honest with yourself about how you feel when you are in one, and when you are out of one. Hold space for the realizations that you can be yourself and stay true to your path, even in a relationship.

Scorpio North Node | Taurus South Node

Your journey this lifetime is to allow yourself to transform. With your South Node in Taurus, you tend to resist change. You stubbornly hold onto behaviors which are no longer serving you because they are comfortable. Challenge yourself on this Eclipse to step away from all of your comfort zones. Notice what emotions arise when you think about venturing into the unfamiliar and hold space for them to pass. Recognize the potential of the unknown and allow yourself to break down to breakthrough.

Sagittarius North Node | Gemini South Node

Your journey this lifetime is to expand. This can be through travel, living in new cities, meeting new people, or exposing yourself to new knowledge. With your South Node in Gemini, you tend to focus on the details of your life instead of the bigger picture. You find comfort in the intricacies of one energy instead of expanding outward to experience differing vibrations. On this Eclipse, challenge yourself to take a leap of faith and try something new. Take a chance and assume the best will happen.

Capricorn North Node | Cancer South Node

You sit in opposition to this Eclipse, with your North Node in Capricorn. Focus on embracing the higher vibrations of Capricorn this Eclipse while releasing the lower vibrations. Your journey this lifetime is to embrace your work and find joy in sharing your gifts with others. With your South Node in Cancer, you find comfort in self-care, staying home, and giving space to your feelings. While understanding your emotions is a good thing, be cautious not to overindulge in them or allow them to rule your life. On this Eclipse, create containers around your emotions, so you can still experience them, but with boundaries.

Aquarius North Node | Leo South Node

Your journey this lifetime is to express your voice on a platform that helps move humanity forward. With your South Node in Leo, you find comfort in expressing your uniqueness. You are a natural leader, but in this lifetime, it's more important for you to be part of a team, equal to everyone. On this Eclipse, feel into your compassionate nature and extend it out to everyone you meet. Find ways to shift your frequency through understanding your emotions. Become aware of how that changes the frequency of the space around you.

Pisces North Node | Virgo South Node

You are on a journey this lifetime to expand your consciousness and trust your intuition. With your South Node in Virgo, you tend to focus on perfectionism and find comfort in an organized life. This lifetime, though, is about finding, and embracing chaos. Instead of seeking definition, see everything as one without distinction between your energy and the world around you. On the Eclipse, challenge yourself to feel the interconnectedness of everything. Realize that you, and your emotions, are not separate from one another. In this complete merger of energies, you'll find the deep healing.

CANCER LUNAR FLOW

The Full Moon in Cancer is a time to settle into ourselves and allow our body to unravel. We often hold suppressed emotions in our muscles and connective tissue, which contribute to our feelings of emotional attachment. To allow our emotions to flow freely, we need to release our body and the energy it holds. The following sequence is a Yin sequence, which relies on longer holds than a typical yoga practice. In holding postures, we are able to release into the pose fully, and allow our body to unwind completely. In each pose, focus on your breath and use it to keep your mind clear, as your body lets go of tension. Also, have support ready in the form of a blanket, bolster, and blocks. When we have support physically or mentally, we are more likely to release and let go of tension.

To begin, come to a seated posture, sitting on a blanket or a bolster. Have a timer handy, and set it for 3 minutes. During these first minutes, focus solely on your breath. On the inhale, count to 4, on exhale count back down from 4. Continue this counting for the remaining time. This is the pace of the breath for the entire practice. Use the numbers to help focus your mind and keep it from wandering away from the present moment.

Baddha Konasana // Cobblers Pose: 5 minutes

Bring your feet together with your knees out to either side for Baddha Konasana. Prop your hips up on a blanket if needed. You can also place blocks, under your knees for support. Gently fold over your legs and allow your back and neck to relax. Once you are in a Yin pose, hold it and breathe. There is less emphasis on alignment in these types of poses versus vinyasa or Hatha postures. Continue to count up to four and back down from four as you breathe, and allow your body to unwind. If you are met with resistance in any area, try sending your breath to that area and asking it gently to open up.

CANCER LUNAR FLOW

Janu Sirsana // One-legged forward fold: 3 minutes each side

Extend your legs out long on the mat. Sit on top of a blanket and take your right foot to the inside of the left leg. Fold over your front leg. You can have your blocks stacked by your leg to support your forehead as you fold. Allow your spine to round and your head to be heavy. Relax your leg, and let the foot be soft. Breathe here for 3 minutes, allowing your hamstrings to open, sending your breath into this area. Slowly switch sides, giving yourself and your body time to unwind in the transition.

Ardha Apanasana (Supported) // One-legged Knee to Chest pose - 3 minutes each side

Lie on your back and have your bolster nearby. Place the bolster, or block, under your hips, propping you up into a slight backbend. Hug your right knee into your chest and stretch your left leg long. Feel an opening in your left hip as you breathe here for 3 minutes. Let go of tension in your shoulders and your neck. On each exhale, feel your body sink into the floor a bit more. After 3 minutes, slowly switch sides.

Setu Bandhasana (Supported) // Bridge Pose: 3-5 minutes

While on your back, bend your knees and have your feet hip-width apart. Have your blocks nearby. On inhale, lift your hips into bridge pose. Place two blocks under your hips, feeling your entire body supported. Allow yourself to rest entirely on the blocks. Have your arms by your side, and place slight pressure on your triceps pressing the floor away to open the chest. Release the pressure and focus solely on your breath for 3 -5 minutes. On each exhale, let go of tension in your neck and shoulders. Once the time is complete, slowly remove the blocks and set your back down one vertebra at a time, pausing at the bottom.

Supported Fish Pose: 5 minutes

You can either use a bolster or two blocks for this pose. If using a bolster, place it lengthwise on your mat and lay over it, with it supporting your spine and head. If using two blocks, which is a deeper pose, place one block on the tallest height for your head, then the other block lengthwise, so it fits in between your shoulder blades. Lying on both blocks, or the bolster, either place your legs into Baddha Konasana or have them straight on the mat. Place your palms upward in a receptive position and feel your entire body relax. Allow your heart and chest to expand and feel into the vulnerability of this position. Know you are safe and supported. Allow yourself to fully receive the gifts of this pose and the new energy flooding into your being.

Supine Twist: 3 minutes each side

Remain on your back. Hug your left knee into your chest once again and twist to the right side. You can place your bolster or block under this knee to give support to your twist. Stretch your right arm out to the side, but keep the neck neutral. Fill your low back with your breath as you breathe, releasing more into the twist on each exhale. After 3 minutes, slowly come up and switch sides.

Savasana: 5 minutes

Stretch your legs out long on the mat. Have your palms facing upward in a receptive motion. Allow your entire weight to be supported by the floor beneath you as you rest. Let go of the counting of the breath and breathe naturally, observing the quiet flow of inhale and exhale.

inhale *exhale*

LUNAR ECLIPSE MEDITATION

The following meditation is a version of mindfulness meditation to help you regulate and balance your emotions. Take your time with this one, and only do it for as long as you feel comfortable. If emotions become too intense at any point, know you can always rest in the breath.

Begin in a comfortable seated position or lying down, fully supporting your body. Close your eyes and begin to first breathe into your belly. Expand your abdomen with each breath, filling up like a balloon. Exhale completely, deflating your lungs and stomach. Breathe like this for one minute, calming your entire nervous system. When you feel ready, begin to notice what emotions are present in your body. This can be anything from irritation to joy, sadness, or even contentment. Acknowledge any feelings that are present in your field and label them, giving them definition. Just observe what they are for a moment, then begin to scan your body, feeling for physical sensations associated with a particular emotion.

Locate the space where you hold your emotions and feel the sensations that are associated with them. This may be tightness, heaviness, or any other sensation. Without trying to change anything, observe which bodily sensations arise when you experience certain emotions. Bring your awareness to the strongest sensation in your body. Create an outline, or container around that sensation, isolating it from the rest of your body. Become fully aware that this sensation does not make up your entire being, but instead occupies only a part of your energetic and bodily field. Once you have the emotion and corresponding sensation contained, breathe into the container filling it with energy and love. Continue to breathe into this space and notice what new sensations arise. Do this without trying to change what already exists within you. Simply bear witness to your feelings. Allow new sensations to develop and be felt. This may bring up fear, other feelings, or may just make you feel lighter in your body. Anything that occurs is exactly the right thing for this moment. Continue breathing into your container, giving your body and energy time to process the emotion. Continue holding space for your emotions, letting them move freely, shift, and change. Know that they will pass, and every sensation we feel is temporary, even if it feels like it isn't in the moment. Through bringing awareness and compassion to your emotions, you give it the chance to release from your field.

Continue breathing into your container for 5 minutes, or longer if you like. Stay fully present with yourself through the process. Do not rush yourself, or force a release before it is ready. Also, do not overthink your emotions. Just stay present with them and give them space to breathe. When you're finished with the feeling, dissolve the container and allow that part of you to integrate back into the rest of your field. Bring your attention back to your breath in your belly. Continue to practice abdominal breathing for another minute, re-centering yourself.

Lunar Eclipse

STEP BY STEP RITUAL

1 GRAB A BROKEN CRYSTAL, SHELL, ROCK, SOMETHING ORGANIC FROM THE EARTH

2 HOLD IT AND MENTALLY SEND NEGATIVE ENERGY INTO THE ROCK

3 THANK THE ENERGY FOR THE LESSONS IT HAS TAUGHT YOU.

4 FINALLY, SAY GOODBYE TO THIS ENERGY. RELEASE IT INTO A BODY OF WATER, AND LET GO.

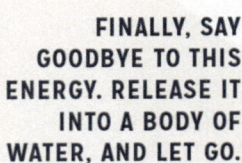

CANCER CIRCLE

This Lunar Eclipse is a powerful time to align with yourself and your community. You can choose to practice alone or with others, but try to practice the rituals in this workbook during some part of the Lunar Eclipse. If you miss this window, it's ok, try to practice while the Moon is still in Cancer. Choose a quiet location to set up your Moon Circle, either inside or outside. This powerful Eclipse incorporates the energies of all the elements; Fire, Air, Water, and Earth. Bring them in through various tools. For air, include auric sprays, feathers to fan the smudge sticks, and even wind chimes to hear the air moving around you. Choose candles to represent fire or build an outside fire. Bring in the element of water through a room diffuser, a vase with flowers in it, or just a simple silver metal bowl containing water. You can use crystals to represent the Earth element. Crystals that align with this Eclipse are; Selenite for intuition. Tiger's eye to feel your power. Rose quartz to align with unconditional love. Malachite to help transmute and dissolve the Ego. Lemurian Quartz to help download universal knowledge, and Moldavite to facilitate expansion into higher planes of consciousness. Gather all of your supplies and start to build your circle.

Once you've built your circle, use a smudge stick of sage or palo santo to clean the space and everyone in it. Use your intuitive guidance when leading yourself and others. Start by giving space for everyone to introduce themselves and any energy they are calling into the circle. Discuss how you are feeling with the energy of the day, then practice the meditation and/or yoga together. Before beginning the practice section in this workbook, perform the letting go ritual written below, to make space for new energy to integrate into your field.

Release Ritual:
This ritual is a practice in letting go. It's best done at the time of the Lunar Eclipse, but can be practiced at any time the day of the Eclipse. It gives us something physical to contain our unwanted energies, and gives us a representation of what it feels like to let something completely detach from our field. Pick an object to discard; this can be a pebble or rock, something organic in nature as you will be throwing it into a body of water. If you do not live near an ocean or stream, pick a small organic object that will fit in a drainage grate. Take your object and go to a body of water, like the ocean, a river, just something that will carry the object away from you, so not your bathtub.a

Hold the object in your hand, and think about all the things you are ready to let go. These things can be anger, pain, or hurt feelings. They can be specific to a person or situation, or they can be general. Mentally, send all of the energies into the object you are holding. Feel them leave your field and attach to the object's field. Once you've placed all the energies you wish to discard into the object, take a deep breath and on exhale, throw it into the body of water. Know that the water will cleanse the energy and bring it back to the Earth, where it will be composted or eroded into something new. Know that this practice will free you of the energetic binds and will create space within you for new creations.

Once you've released what no longer serves you, begin to work with the questions in this workbook. You can share your answers out loud with the group or keep them to yourself. Enjoy the exchange of energy this night brings you. You can even practice pulling from your favorite deck of cards and asking the universe what energy is needed for you to shift into a higher state of consciousness. End your circle by giving gratitude to everyone who participated and give appreciation to yourself for showing up.

CANCER CARD READING

Reading Cards is a beautiful way to access your intuition and tap into your, and the Universe's, higher wisdom. Anyone can pull cards, as long as you are willing to receive the information they provide. You need no prior experience, or training, just an open and clear mind.

You may use any cards you like for this practice, including but not limited to: Tarot Cards, Animal Medicine Cards, Oracle Cards or any Affirmation Cards. You also can pull cards from a few decks to gain different perspectives. If you are new to card pulling, try to ask only one deck the same question, as asking different decks the same question can become quite confusing. Below are some general guidelines on how to pull cards. Please improvise as needed and above anything else, listen to your intuition.

Clear your mind
A settled, grounded mind is essential for pulling cards. The last thing you want is random thoughts running around when you are trying to receive clear answers from yourself. Practice the breath work and meditation in this workbook to prepare and settle your mind. You may also clear your mind using sound frequencies through singing bowls. These can either be crystal or metal bowls. Play the bowl, or bowls, for about 3-5 minutes to help rid your mind of external noise as you focus on the harmony of the sound.

CANCER CARD READING

Pick your deck

There are many different decks out there. You can choose as many as you like. Know, though, that they each provide you a different energy or medicine. Tarot Cards are the most popular and should be used carefully. Although very useful, Tarot cards can give the wrong impression if you interpret them harshly. Animal Medicine cards offer different types of messages from the animal realm which can help align with the spirit of nature. These cards give you the medicine you need to apply to your situation or question. Affirmation cards provide you with guidance in the form of words or phrases. When reading these cards, it is best to meditate on what the affirmation means for you. It is also helpful to repeat the affirmation a few times and see how it makes you feel. There are many other cards you can experiment with, like Goddess Cards, Angel Cards, and so on. The important thing to remember with any card is that they each have different angles and sides. There are often a few interpretations of the same card.

Shuffle

Shuffle the cards the easiest way for you. Some cards are smaller and can be shuffled like a regular deck of playing cards, while others with take some effort. If all else fails, spread them out on the floor in front of you then regather them. Keep a clear mind while shuffling. You can also repeat " I am open to receiving guidance and intuition." Refrain from asking your questions until the next step.

Cancer Card Questions

You are free to ask the deck any questions you need answers to on this Lunar Eclipse. The following questions are meant to help you harness the energy of Cancer through the cards to clarify some of these energies in your mind. This is a three-part card reading, where you'll ask the deck three questions. Before beginning, spread your freshly shuffled cards in a wide arc in front of you. Use your left middle finger to choose the card, first waving your hand slowly over the cards. You'll feel a magnetic pull, or slight tingle, in your fingertip when you hover over the right card. Chose one card at a time, taking a moment to breathe in between questions. Keep the cards flipped over until you pull all three.

1. *What energy will help me release struggle in my life?*
2. *What energy will help me feel and understand my emotions more deeply?*
3. *What energy will help me create a life full of ease and joy aligned with my soul?*

Take Them In

Once you have your cards, flip them over. Before looking up their meaning, sit with them for a moment and allow them to speak to you. Intuit your own meaning and interpretation of the card. What is the card trying to tell you? What are you trying to tell yourself? After a few moments with the cards, look up their meaning. Sit with that information, merging it with your intuitive meaning of the cards.

As with everything, enjoy this process. Do not worry if you are doing it right or wrong. Just follow your intuition, and trust the journey. Accept the cards you are dealt and use their energy wisely to help guide you when you need it the most.

"From the chaos of her heart flowed the power of her intuition."

- spirit daughter

CANCER PRACTICES

When we look at the energies of Cancer and Capricorn, we see on one side how we nurture ourselves and on the opposite side, how we nurture other people. The opportunity this Eclipse is to find a balance between these energies. If we align too heavily with the vibrations of Cancer, we incorporate plenty of self-care into our lives but end up hiding our talents. To protect our energy, we may not share it with other people. This need to protect ourselves can make us miss an opportunity to feel helpful and fulfilled.

At the other extreme, when we align too heavily with the energies of Capricorn, we may forgo taking care of ourselves in an effort to give our talents to others. In most cases, this shows up as a desire to work long hours, or sacrifice precious self-care for recognition or career advancement. To prove our abilities, we forget our first responsibility is to nurture ourselves. This type of behavior takes away the joy in our work, as we simply go through the motions, forgetting to honor our soul.

When we balance the extreme side of Cancer and Capricorn, we balance our life and our work. We understand when to take time for ourselves and when to give our time to others. We also understand what brings us joy, including how to incorporate that joy into our career. Our work then begins to flow as all the pieces line up effortlessly. When in this rhythm, we realize that life does not have to include struggle. Our work does not have to be hard to be fulfilling, and success does not have to come at the price of our well being. With a true work-life balance, we can have it all, and we can have it all with ease.

Once we realize that our life can include time for ourselves and time for our work, the universe rearranges our world to include this vision. Getting to this place energetically, though, requires we release the notion that life is "either, or." We often think we can have one thing, like self-care, or another, like success at work. We find it hard to include the possibility that we can have both. Stretch your perspective this Eclipse to include a vision that includes all aspects of a balanced work- life. Realize that you can take care of yourself while being successful. You can have a fulfilling career, aligned with your soul without sacrificing your relationships. You also can experience joy and restoration while pursuing your life's work.

The key to a balanced life is to create a life that restores you on every level. This includes carving out time for self-care, time for relationships, and time to share your talents in the form of work. Every piece of your life can be aligned with your soul and your true essence, once you understand it. On this Lunar, Eclipse, focus on learning about yourself at a fundamental level. Feel what nurtures you and brings you restoration. Feel what fulfills you. This may be a night spent in the tub journaling, but it also might be finishing a project which allows you to share yourself with others. Your work can be just as restorative as a day at the spa if it aligns with your soul. Likewise, spending time with the people you love can also recharge your battery. Also, realize that you have enough time for all of these things. It is possible to have a life which includes everything which fulfills your soul- and it can be easy.

CANCER PRACTICES

1. What restores your energy? This can be anything from a day spent in nature to a night working on a project until 3am.

CANCER PRACTICES

2. What depletes your energy?

_____

_____

_____

_____

_____

_____

_____

_____

_____

_____

_____

_____

_____

_____

_____

_____

_____

_____

_____

_____

_____

_____

CANCER PRACTICES

3. When you feel depleted, how is your intuition affected?

CANCER PRACTICES

4. How do you give space for your feelings to emerge? Do you
   need more of this space or less of it to help balance your life?

_____

_____

_____

_____

_____

_____

_____

_____

_____

_____

_____

_____

_____

_____

_____

_____

_____

_____

_____

_____

_____

_____

_____

_____

_____

CANCER PRACTICES

5. What brings you joy? Meaning what makes you feel fulfilled
    and truly happy at your core?

CANCER PRACTICES

6. How can you nourish this joy? Meaning what are some activities you can do which enhance it, make it a priority and help you create a life full of it?

_____

_____

_____

_____

_____

_____

_____

_____

_____

_____

_____

_____

_____

_____

_____

_____

_____

_____

_____

_____

_____

_____

_____

_____

_____

CANCER PRACTICES

7. What parts of your life align with your joy? What parts take away from it?

CANCER PRACTICES

8. What are some of your "either/or" statements? Meaning in what ways do you limit yourself from having it all by telling yourself you can have "this" or "that?"

_____

_____

_____

_____

_____

_____

_____

_____

_____

_____

_____

_____

_____

_____

_____

_____

_____

_____

_____

_____

_____

_____

_____

_____

CANCER PRACTICES

9. In what ways may you be addicted to struggle? This can show up as always being "too busy" or always stating that life is hard, or that there is too much happening right now.

CANCER PRACTICES

10. How can you have it all without feeling like any of it is a struggle? This is a larger vision which can take years to manifest but as we venture into 2020 try to expand your perceptions to include a life full of everything which brings you joy without having to work as hard to obtain it. Envision a balanced life where your work restores you, your relationships fulfill you, and your time alone helps you align with your intuition which leads you forward in your life with ease and grace.

LAST QUARTER

JANUARY 17TH | LIBRA

Last Quarter Moons provide an energy of release, a time to clear the field before we reset with the New Moon in one week. This release, though, generally comes after a crisis or breakdown. When the Moon is half full, it is squaring (90-degree separation) the Sun. Square aspects feel tense; they pull on our energy and can make us feel irritable. Their tension can inspire a breakthrough, though, where we can see a different perspective and surrender an old notion or way of life.

This Last Quarter Moon in Libra squares the Sun in Capricorn, bringing up questions around our relationships and our focus. It's a time to look at your relationships and decide which ones nourish you and which ones may be distracting you from your journey. Libra is a sign of balance. Align with this energy to bring balance to your partnerships and ensure they align with your soul and what brings you joy.

Last Quarter Moons are a time to finish some of the work started on the Full Moon. It'sIt's a final chance to let go of energies that do not serve us in integrating the higher vibrations of Cancer and Capricorn. Think back to some of the realizations you may have had on the Lunar Eclipse. Revisit some of the emotions that arose and the revelations you had about them. Apply what you learned to your partnerships. First, gain some clarity about how you really feel about them and how they support you emotionally. Which relationships help you to explore your feelings and which ones suppress them? Furthermore, which ones help you honor and listen to your intuition and which ones silence it? Or make it impossible for you to follow it?

As you explore your relationships, ask yourself which ones feel like too much work. All relationships require a degree of effort on both parties to help them evolve and grow, but are there any which feel one-sided? Meaning, do any of them feel like you are doing all the work to nourish them and keep them meaningful? Additionally, do any of these relationships take up too much of your time, not leaving room for other pieces of your life to flourish. Take the time this Last Quarter to create some balance in your relationships and ensure they are aligned with your soul and your joy.

What are you willing to let go this Last Quarter Moon to allow yourself to receive new energy?

AFFIRMATIONS

Reflect back to question #8 (pg. 29). Write 3-5 affirmations that oppose your either/or statements. Write affirmations that state you can have it all, whatever that means to you. Notice what thoughts pop up as you do this. You may have doubts about your ability to manifest a truly balanced life, but do not let this discourage you from believing it's possible. Repeat your affirmations every day and let the universe rearrange itself to give you all of your dreams, without having to sacrifice one piece for another.

HAPPY FULL MOON

Thank you to everyone who supported and purchased this workbook.

Special Thanks to Rebecca Reitz (rebeccareitz.com, IG:@becca_reitz) for her beautiful artwork on the cover and pages 2, 4, 6, 14, 32.

For a monthly subscription contact hello@spiritdaughter.com or visit www.spiritdaughter.com

Disclaimer: The exercises and yoga sequences in this book are physical activities that should be performed carefully to avoid injury. You agree to accept all risks and release Spirit Daughter and any guest instructors from any and all liabilities. Please take care and enjoy.